Transforming Your Finances

Wealth Principles from Ancient Wisdom

Table of Contents

Chapter 1. Introduction

Are you ready to unlock the secret to financial prosperity that has stood the test of time? Our Special Report, "Transforming Your Finances: Wealth Principles from Ancient Wisdom," takes a captivating, cheerful journey through age-old financial practices and principles. What if we told you the tools for financial transformation could stem from the scrolls of historical wisdom rather than modern Wall Street strategies? From the grazing grounds of ancient Mesopotamian farmers to the bustling marketplaces of the Roman Empire, this report illuminates the timeless strategies for accruing wealth. As compelling as it is enlightening, it's an investment in knowledge that could fortify your financial future. Take a leap into the annals of finance and unearth the secrets to securing prosperity. With this Special Report, you are one step closer to grasp the lasting wealth principle that never grows old. A brighter and wealthier future awaits - isn't it time your finances time-travelled to prosperity?

Chapter 2. Decoding Wealth in Ancient Civilizations

In the dust-choked corridors of time, we locate the earliest recorded civilizations like Sumer, Egypt, and Indus Valley, where concepts of wealth and financial management first took form. Despite shiny modern accoutrements, contemporary wealth-making principles often echo ancient strategies. Lets first explore the financial acumen of these ancient societies.

2.1. Sumer: The Cradle of Civilization

Sumer (modern-day southern Iraq), dated from 4500 to 1900 BC, was among the world's first civilizations. The civilization's financial prosperity was intrinsically linked to the abundant waters of the Tigris and Euphrates Rivers, resourceful agricultural practices, and early forms of commerce and trade.

Agriculture was the primary driver of wealth in Sumer, enabled by an intricate irrigation system. Sumerians were among the first to introduce crop rotation and control floods for farming, ensuring a reliable food source and surplus crops that could be traded for other goods, services, and even metals, precursors to modern money.

Trade bolstered Sumer's financial prosperity. Although Sumerians lacked easy access to natural resources like timber and metal, they exploited their geographic location advantageously, creating an extensive trading network stretching from the Indus Valley to Egypt and Anatolia. Trade, in turn, facilitated the birth of a primitive form of banking where temples and palace complexes acted as secure sites for the storage of goods and commodities.

Additionally, the invention of Cuneiform, the first writing system, allowed record-keeping, easing the management of assets and transactions. Sumer's financial story was one of innovation and adaptability, valuable lessons for the modern wealth seeker.

2.2. Ancient Egypt: Prosperity Along the Nile

Moving to Ancient Egypt (3150 BC - 31 BC), we find a civilization where wealth was meticulously managed. The Nile River served as the lifeblood of wealth creation, giving rise to a prosperous agrarian economy destined to become a financial behemoth of the ancient world.

Fascinatingly, ancient Egyptians developed a method of taxation, an economic principle still fundamental today. The Pharaoh, as venerated ruler and god, was viewed as the owner of all land, bestowing parcels to subjects in return for taxes, paid chiefly as a proportion of harvested crops. This state-controlled economy ensured wealth distribution, kept granaries full, and facilitated large-scale infrastructural projects.

Trade networks, domestically and across the Red and Mediterranean seas, were vital for Egypt's financial affluence. Key commodities included grain, flax, papyrus, gold, and precious stones, some of which acted as an early form of currency. Wealth generated through this exchange system created an advanced civilization that lasted for millennia, bearing testament to economic foresight.

2.3. Indus Valley Civilization: Masters of Urban Planning

Moving east to the Indus Valley civilization (3300 BC - 1300 BC), enveloping parts of modern-day Pakistan and India, we unveil a society that was astoundingly advanced for its age. A feat demonstrating their exceptional understanding of urban planning, resource allocation, and standardization systems – each vital components of the economic machinery.

The cities of Harappa and Mohenjo-Daro exhibited grid-like structures, extensive drainage systems, and uniform brick sizes – indicative of planning, regulation, and standardization, hallmarks of modern city planning. These factors invited wealth by paving the path for efficient trade, solidifying the civilization's economic standing.

Indus Valley citizens were active traders, with extensive networks reaching as far as Mesopotamia. The uniformity noted in weights and measures speaks volumes on their grasp of standards and fair trade principles, aspects central to any successful trading economy.

Their economic acumen is underscored by the discovery of seals, perhaps used for marking ownership or transactions, akin to the terracotta tokens Sumerians used to denote goods or services.

The Indus Valley civilization's fall remains shrouded in mystery. Yet, their tale - abundant in planning and standardization - underlies time-tested principles applicable to today's wealth creation and economy.

Ancient civilizations' enduring legacies provide financial lessons for contemporary seekers of prosperity. From close-to-nature agrarian models to methods of fair trade, taxation, resource allocation, and urban planning, our forebears hold solutions for today's economic challenges. With this newfound appreciation, we realize that wealth and financial management aren't strictly modern concepts but echo historical practices, tested and honed over millennia. History humbles us with the revelation that we aren't the first to explore these matters and suggests that the answers we seek for financial prosperity are flowing in the river, engraved on walls, and buried in our fertile past. Embracing these lessons ensures we can remain in tune with wealth strategies that have weathered the sands of time.

Chapter 3. The Shepherds' Secret: Agrarian Wealth Principles

Long before the millennia of stock markets, internet trading, or even money, there existed wealth. It was a wealth measured not in coins but in fields of gold - golden wheat, that is - and the flocks that roamed these fields. Today, we delve into the wisdom that dates back thousands of years, imparted by none other than the first custodians of wealth – the shepherds.

3.1. The Pastoral Economy: Shepherd's Path to Wealth

Anchored in simplicity, the pastoral way of life fostered a rudimentary yet powerful form of wealth creation. Agrarian communities, specifically shepherd economies, developed sophisticated mechanisms for managing risk, creating value, and generating wealth.

Shepherds tended livestock, sheep in most instances. Sheep offered milk, wool, and meat, which made them one of your primary assets. Crop farming provided a secondary source of income, but livestock was primal. Therefore, your wealth was based on the size and health of your flock – the more sheep you had, the wealthier you were considered.

Yet, the numerical strength of the flock was just one determinant of wealth. The other crucial element was stewardship. You needed to secure your sheep against diseases, predators, and harsh weather. Resourcefulness connected to the availability of pastures and water resources was also vital. A wealthy shepherd was not merely one possessing a large flock, but also one who could keep his herd healthy and thriving.

3.2. Safeguarding Your Income: Risk Management

The task of shepherding posed various challenges which, by necessity, shepherds transformed into learning opportunities. Predators posed a constant threat. Shepherds had to predict potential risks based on weather patterns, the animals' behavior, and predatory patterns. They had to build shelters and devise defenses, exhibiting an early form of risk management.

The nomadic lifestyle also served as a form of risk management. By continuously moving their flocks, shepherds could reduce overgrazing and potential resource exhaustion. They safeguarded their means of income by rotating pasturelands, reflecting an ancient wisdom about the preservation of natural resources that is incredibly pertinent even today.

3.3. Multiplying Wealth: Reinvestment

Wealth multiplication in agrarian societies rested on the principle of reinvestment. For shepherds, this took the form of nurturing their flock. Keeping a part of the flock's produce for their survival and allowing for natural growth was key.

Reinvestment resources were not strictly monetary. Instead, it was time, care, and participation in the flock's growth. This principle showed that constant and careful reinvestment could steadily multiply wealth. This timeless strategy continues to find a place in contemporary investment theories, which advocate for the regular, calculated reinvestment of earnings.

3.4. Inclusion and Equality: Wealth Redistribution

Even in those early societies, they practiced a form of wealth distribution. Unlike contemporary systems where wealth concentration often leads to power concentration, shepherd societies relied on each member receiving a fair share.

Shepherds' communities operated on a principle of mutual aid, where they helped one another during hard times. This distributed wealth, reduced risk, and prevented power concentration. This principle underlines the importance of social responsibilities in enforcing economic equality — an age-old concept that forms the backbone of many modern wealth redistribution policies.

3.5. The key to Resilient Wealth: Adaptability

Shepherds inherently understood the need for adaptability to survive. They adapted to changing seasons, migration patterns, and the variable availability of resources.

The connection between wealth and adaptability is equally valid today. With advances in technology, changing economic circumstances, and unpredictable events, adaptability remains vital for safeguarding and growing wealth. The need for prudent financial planning, flexibility, innovation, and a willingness to change tactics aligns directly with the hard-learned lessons of ancient shepherds.

These shepherd's secrets, born out of necessity and honed over generations of pastoral life, remain invaluable. They underline core principles of finance — managing risk, reinvesting income, redistributing wealth, and adapting to change. Unveiling and appreciating these principles can help us build a foundation for modern financial prosperity. The wisdom hoarded by our shepherd forebears, rooted in the simplicity of their lifestyle, holds a transformative power that has the potential to redefine our relationship with wealth.

Chapter 4. Trading and Commerce: Lessons from Phoenician Merchants

The Phoenician civilization, centered around present-day Lebanon, was one of the most influential ancient cultures, known for their seafaring skills and commercial acumen. Discerning lessons from their prosperous trading and commerce strategies could unlock bountiful dividends.

4.1. The Phoenician Trade Network

The Phoenicians established an expansive and efficient trade network, stretching from Mesopotamia to Spain. This network, fueled by their superior navigational capabilities, was integral to their economic success. Trade was their bloodline and they sought out commodity-rich regions, establishing colonies and trade connections that ushered in prosperity.

Their efficiency lay in their ships, unsurpassed in speed and capacity. These aptly named "ships of Tarshish" could navigate the open sea and shallow waters alike, making them ideal for the varied coastal and river port conditions. Their outrigger design provided stability, enabling them to transport heavy goods without jeopardizing speed or navigability.

Understanding the structure, reach, and efficiency of their trade network sets the groundwork for appreciating the broader principles at play.

4.2. The Value of Commodities

The Phoenicians are revered for their purple textiles, coined "Tyrian purple." This expensive, labor-intensive dye became a symbol of wealth, command, and regality, contributing significantly to their economic prosperity.

The underlying principle here involves identifying unique, high-value commodities that are in demand and monopolizing their production and supply. Their trade network allowed the Phoenicians to export Tyrian purple to the far reaches of the known world, maximizing their profits.

4.3. Risk Management in Trading

Phoenician merchants were not immune to risks. Maritime perils, political unrest, and market fluctuations were everyday occurrences. However, they skillfully managed these risks, distributing their trade across regions and commodities.

This risk mitigation strategy is vital, even today. Modern portfolio theory advocates similar principles - diversify to reduce risk while maximizing expected returns.

4.4. Building and Maintaining Relationships

The Phoenicians mastered the art of building and maintaining relationships. They acquitted themselves as trustworthy trade partners, ensuring a mutually beneficial commerce mechanism. Diplomatic ties bolstered by intermarriage became commonplace to solidify alliances and secure trade routes.

This lesson transcends time; successful business hinges on

relationships grounded in trust and mutual benefits. It is an essential foundation of modern networking principles and strategic partnerships.

4.5. Currency and Standardization

One of the lesser acknowledged feats of the Phoenicians was their standardization of trade weights, measures, and coinage. This paved the way for more effective commerce, establishing trusted scales for exchange and reducing the potential for conflict or misunderstanding.

Modern business practices still bear the imprint of this innovation. Today's standardized currency systems and globally accepted units of measurements vitalize international trade and commerce.

Chapter 5. Innovation for Competitive Advantage

The development of the Phoenician alphabet is a testament to their innovative spirit. To streamline record-keeping and communication, the merchants of Phoenicia developed an alphabet that was simple to learn and write. It expedited effective communication and transformed information dissemination across the trade network.

This fundamental principle remains strikingly relevant. Innovation, aimed at simplifying processes or solving challenges, presents lucrative competitive advantages.

By embracing these potent lessons from Phoenician merchants - cultivating efficient networks, identifying and leveraging value commodities, managing risks through diversification, nurturing strong professional relationships, maintaining standardization for transparency, and fostering innovation, one can unlock unprecedented financial gains, echoing the prosperous frequencies of ancient wisdom in contemporary economic landscapes.

Chapter 6. The Roman Affluence: Probing into the Empire's Financial Mastery

The Roman Republic, and subsequently the Roman Empire, were geopolitical entities distinguished by a sophisticated and diverse economy. Comparable to the most advanced economies of the modern Western world, the Roman finance system demonstrated an extraordinary level of complexity and versatility.

6.1. Roman Currency and Economic Activity

The Roman economy employed a vast network of coins for trade and commerce, unlike the earlier simplistic barter systems. The denarius, minted from nearly pure silver, was the most commonly used currency throughout the Empire.

An intricate banking system supported these financial activities. The argentarii (money changers) and mensarii (bankers) conducted money lending and exchange activities, dealing with large sums and transactions across the Empire. The Roman financial system also demonstrated an understanding of credit and debt, allowing loans to be made and debts to be sold.

6.2. The Importance of Trade

Trade was an indispensable part of the Roman Empire's economy. Grain from Egypt, wild animals from Africa, silk from China - Rome's trade connections spanned across continents. Import and export agreements were crucial, as they helped feed the gargantuan demands of the Roman populace and ensured the supply of luxury goods and exotic items for the aristocracy.

Roman merchants showcased resilience and adaptability, risking long voyages to ensure the smooth flow of goods. Roman law aided this process, providing a robust framework of contract law and property rights that facilitated and protected trade.

6.3. Infrastructure and Public Works

Roman prosperity was achieved not only through currency and trade but also through immense public works and infrastructure projects. Monumental structures like the Colosseum, aqueducts, roads, and buildings across the Empire were not mere displays of grandeur, but they fueled the economy through construction, maintenance, and subsequent jobs they created or supported.

Empire-wide connectivity enabled by Roman roads and sea routes facilitated the movement of both goods and labor, boosting the economic well-being of the Empire. Aqueducts and water systems ensured the health of the populous and their livestock, reinforcing the productive potential of Roman society.

6.4. Taxation in the Roman Empire

The Romans had a comprehensive and efficient taxation system, which funded the vast administrative machinery of the Empire and supported the Roman army. Tax levels were often high, but they provided the necessary resources to maintain security, infrastructure, and public services.

Provincial taxation often took the form of a direct levy on people or their properties. Revenue was used to maintain the local infrastructure, fund the municipal governments, and provide for the

Imperial court and the military.

6.5. Slavery and the Roman Economy

Arguably, slavery was the dark underbelly of the Roman economic system. A captured prisoner-of-war, a bought slave, or a born serf would often perform the bulk of labor-intensive tasks in the Roman economy, from tilling the fields to manning the oars of galleys, to building the grand Roman structures.

Despite the profound ethical issues associated with slavery, it was an integral part of the Roman economy. The impact of this forced labor on Roman productivity and wealth accumulation cannot be underestimated.

6.6. Economic Policies and Financial Crises

Like any modern economy, the Roman Empire wasn't immune to volatility and had its fair share of financial crises. Hyperinflation, economic downturns, high taxes, corruption, and tepid fiscal responses plagued the Empire at times. Emperors reacted with remedies that ranged from debasement of the currency to social welfare policies.

However, these crises were often short-lived. The economy's resilience and adaptability, honed by centuries of Roman administrative expertise, allowed it to weather economic storms and maintain long-term stability and prosperity.

6.7. The Legacy of Roman Economic System

The Roman Empire left a profound and enduring economic legacy. Its innovative financial practices, efficient administrative systems, and far-sighted economic policy and governance laid the foundation for many modern financial systems. While modern economies have far surpassed the complexity and sophistication of the Roman system, the echoes of Roman financial mastery can still be heard today in our principles of trade, currency, infrastructure development, and public finance.

In conclusion, the prosperity of the Roman Empire was not the result of a single factor but a combination of financial innovation, efficient administration, robust infrastructure, and expansive trade. While modern-day financial strategies may seem far removed from those of ancient Rome, the principles underlying Roman prosperity still hold relevance in today's context as we strive for a brighter and wealthier future.

Chapter 7. Debt, Loans, and Interest: Insights from Babylonian Finance

Babylon, a city-state that flourished nearly 4000 years ago inMesopotamia (modern-day Iraq) holds an element of truly ancient wisdom for us - the first known financial inscriptions pertaining to debt, loans, and interest. A place and time far removed from our modern economies, yet, the principles unearthed from this epoch have an uncanny relevance even today.

7.1. The Nature of Debt in Ancient Babylon

One of the first things to understand about ancient Babylonian society is that debt was considered a normal part of life. It was neither seen as an ill omen nor a roadblock on incursions to wealth. It was a simple economic tool employed by people to navigate their day-to-day life. Babylonian debt structure was rooted in a barter system, often entailing exchanges of goods or services over time - a farmer, for instance, might receive seeds and tools in spring, pledging to repay the debt after harvest.

From extant ancient cuneiform tablets, economists and historians have discerned the fundamental principles Babylonians abided by. They understood the concept of balance, and though they lived in a simpler economy, they maintained disciplined financial habits. They taught us the first principle - never allow debt to linger. It was common to settle debts as quickly as possible after the harvest season, thus avoiding the accumulation of interest.

7.2. The Development of Loans

As trade expanded and agglomerated, the Babylonians began to use silver as a medium of exchange, a precursor of money. Loans too, came into existence, facilitating a range of practical scenarios - buying farmland, funding trade expeditions, or addressing emergencies such as famine. Loans were thus not the spawns of recklessness or need, but a tool for opportunity and contingency.

Tabulations on clay tablets indicate that loans were usually formalised through contracts. Interest rates, collaterals and payment terms were meticulously defined, and failure to repay loans could lead to severe penalties, including enslavement. Thus, the second principle dawned - a loan is a commitment and should not be taken lightly.

The Babylonians introduced a different kind of loan known as the commercial loan. Here, the moneylender not only provided the money but also shared the risky venture with the borrower. The concept of sharing risk is a distinguishing trait of Babylonian finance that we still hang onto today.

7.3. Emergence of the Interest System

Alongside the proliferation of loans, the concept of interest sprung up in Babylonian society. The word used for interest, *mash*, literally meant "calf." This denoted the idea of multiplication, akin to how a herd grows over time.

Interest was thus seen as a tool for wealth multiplication. It was charged on loans of silver and produce, effectively providing moneylenders with an incentive to lend. The widely accepted rate of interest was 20%, a steep climb for the modern sensibility, but justifiable, considering the risks involved in lending during that epoch. This handover of cash resembled the sowing of seeds; it demystified the third principle - the potential for wealth lies in the seeds sown today.

However, high-interest rates also meant the potential for unpayable debts. To obviate such outcomes, the ancient Babylonians implemented laws to control the spread. The Code of Hammurabi, one of the oldest deciphered writings of significant length in the world, contains several laws related to loans and interest. Many of these laws were designed to protect borrowers, demonstrating a keen sense of social justice that lay at the heart of Babylonian finance.

7.4. Final Thoughts: Babylonian Parallels in Today's Time

The principles of old Babylon – using debt wisely, repaying loans promptly, and understanding the nature of interest – sit at the heart of modern finance. Despite the vast temporal and societal differences, these principles still resonate, offering us a roadmap to navigate our financial journeys.

Realizing the importance of paying off debt quickly can save us from high interest rates and financial insecurity. Recognizing that taking on loans is a commitment can help us weigh risks and opportunities judiciously. And understanding the potential for wealth growth through sensible investment can guide us to financial prosperity.

So, take this journey back to ancient Babylon as a learning excursion, and bring back these time-tested finance principles and strategies into your present. Subtle shifts in your financial approach, guided by these long-ago principles, can fortify your economic resilience, progressively leading you to a stage of enduring prosperity. The financial wisdom of Babylon certainly stands the test of time and offers a far-sighted lens for viewing and managing our financial lives today.

Chapter 8. Precious Metals: Early Forms of Wealth and Currency

Many believe the concept of currency sprouted in contemporary times. Yet, tracing its roots, one finds a story of trade that began with commodity bartering which eventually evolved to standardized tokens: the precious metals. Gold, silver, copper, and other such metals wouldn't just act as indications of wealth and status, but came to serve essential functions in the economy.

8.1. The Genesis of Precious Metal Use

It's no coincidence that precious metals became synonymous with wealth. Their rarity, malleability, and durability made them valuable assets. Early humans soon realized that these metals could be formed into various shapes and designs, making them ideal for crafting jewelry and adornments, a primitive form of demonstrating wealth and prestige. Yet, the transformation from decorative artifacts to a medium of exchange represented a significant leap in human civilization.

The Neolithic Revolution, a period marking the shift from hunting-gathering to agrarian societies, was fundamental for this leap. With the advent of agriculture, humans began to establish more permanent settlements, leading to the increase in trade and commercial interactions. People needed a form of exchange that transcended the limitations of barter. Precious metals, for their appealing characteristics and universal rarity, fit the bill.

8.2. Creation of Metallic Currency

Standardizing a medium of exchange was crucial to facilitate trade. It enthused order in what had been a situation permeated with an impractical system of bartering. The concept of a standardized medium of exchange, in the form of metallic currency, was born in ancient Mesopotamia around 3000 BCE. It was in these thriving city-states that metal ingots, often in copper or silver, started to be used in commerce. The commodities' mass, denoting their value, was alien to variations in subjective value appraisal, a persistent issue in the barter system.

Soon, other civilizations such as Egypt and India began to adopt similar models, while the Greeks and the Romans further refined this practice by introducing minted coins. Metallic currency enabled traders to port around their wealth, summoning forth the advent of a more global economy.

8.3. From Metals to Minted Coins

Initially, metals were used in their raw form, but this form of currency had its challenges. The worth of any piece of metal was initially determined by its weight. Thus, it necessitated the presence of scales during each transaction, a tedious and often impractical procedure. Identifying the purity of metals was another problem traders wrestled with.

Minted coins, featuring an emblem or insignia of an issuing authority, offered a convenient solution. Using standardized weights of precious metals like gold, silver, and copper, states minted coins which assured their worth. Lydians, residing in what is now modern-day Turkey, were the first to introduce minted coins around 600 BCE.

8.4. The Value of Gold and Silver

Gold and silver emerged as preferred materials for currency. While copper was also used, its abundance lessened its value. Gold and silver, being scarce, had a superior appeal. Their gleaming finish was symbolic of the sun and moon, revered in many ancient cultures.

Gold offered practical advantages too. It didn't tarnish over time, an important factor when coins could be in circulation for many years, even decades. Silver offered a similar benefit but was less valued due to its relatively higher abundance.

The universal appreciation of gold and silver launched them as global currencies. These metals were cherished from the banks of the Nile to the markets of China, implying that a trader could travel to different parts of the world and find acceptance for their gold and silver coins.

8.5. Socio-Economic Impact of Metallic Currency

The introduction of metal currency had a profound socio-economic impact. Trade became easier and large-scale enterprises could now be feasible. People could amass wealth, fueling social stratification. Kingdoms, too, could accumulate wealth to fund armies and wars.

Middlemen and moneylenders burgeoned, and interest and inflation were introduced. Concepts of debt, credit, and loans emerged. Metallic currency formed the foundation of the basic financial structures that many modern systems continue to use.

Reflecting on the legacy of precious metals as a time-honored form of currency and wealth harbors an understanding of their continued relevance today. Their use transcended from symbolizing personal wealth to becoming a cornerstone of economic structures. The status of gold and silver, especially, as universally recognized assets hasn't diminished; they continue to serve as safe havens in times of economic uncertainty.

From the scrolls of history, it's clear that the understanding, possession, and wise use of precious metals can lead to wealth preservation and growth. Their historic role in trade, commerce, and wealth accumulation offers important wisdom for those seeking financial prosperity. Hence, the principles of investing in precious metals, indeed, stand the test of time. The roots of their value are anchored deep in human civilization and its evolution.

Chapter 9. Ancient China: The Origin of Paper Money and Economic Thought

In the expanse of ancient dynasties and enlightened minds, no civilization encapsulates the genesis of wealth principles as China. The sea of terracotta soldiers, the enduring allure of silk, and the great walls didn't just sprout from soil and stone, but from an intricate understanding of wealth, trade, and economics.

9.1. The Zhou Dynasty: Currency and Commerce

Arguably, the origins of Chinese economic thought can be traced back to the Zhou Dynasty (1046-256 BC). The Zhou represented a significant evolution in China's social and economic structure. People began to settle, plant crops, and build permanent structures. Society gradually transitioned from monarchical rule to feudalism, where power was gradually decentralized, and local lords held sovereignty over their realms.

In this era, the use of standardized coins became prevalent. Made predominantly of bronze, these coins were round with square holes in the middle. This design demonstrated the belief in a round heaven and a square earth, another testimony to the intertwined relationship between spiritual and economic life in China. The introduction of this currency facilitated trading; suddenly, value could be universally recognized and easily transferable, a paradigm shift from the barter system.

9.2. Confucianism and Economic Thought

The period of the Warring States (475-221 BC) that followed after the Zhou Dynasty was turbulent, ripe with socio-political unrest. Amid chaos still managed to bloom one of the most influential thinkers in Chinese history, Confucius. His thoughts and teachings had a profound impact on economic principles.

In Confucianism, the economic system reflects the moral and ethical nature of the people within it. Wealth is not seen as an end in itself but a means to societal harmony, achieved through the ethical conduct of commerce and government. Confucius promoted the idea of "Zhong Yong" or the Doctrine of the Mean, which suggests moderation in all activities, including economic ones. Confucius warned against greed and espoused the principle that one should strive for neither poverty nor riches, but for sufficiency.

9.3. The Birth of Paper Money

Fast forward a few centuries to the Tang Dynasty (618-907 AD). The massive growth in commerce and the corresponding demand for a stable, transportable currency eventually led to the invention of paper money. Surprisingly, this evolution originated from a system used by wealthy individuals and merchants: deposit receipts. People started to deposit their coins with trustworthy agents, receiving a piece of paper indicating their wealth. These papers eventually started to serve as a new currency, as people found it easier to carry and handle.

The government officially regulated paper money only during the Song Dynasty (960-1279 AD), taking advantage of this monetary innovation to solve the issue of copper coin shortage. With these banknotes, named 'jiaozi', the government was now in control of the money supply, a revolution in monetary economics. However, it soon became clear that how this power was wielded could have far-reaching consequences.

9.4. Lessons from the Yuan Dynasty: Hyperinflation

During the Yuan Dynasty's rule (1271-1368 AD), founded by the infamous Kublai Khan, China saw an over-issuance of paper money, resulting in one of the earliest instances of hyperinflation. The overuse of printing press and lack of valuable commodities to back the banknotes led to the devaluation of jiaozi. Prices soared, savings evaporated, and economic stability took a severe hit. This taught us the delicate balance required in maintaining a prosperous economy: just as a lack of money can stifle growth, an oversupply can also lead to disaster.

9.5. Chinese Maritime Trade and the Ming Dynasty

The vibrant economy of the Ming Dynasty (1368-1644 AD) painted a different tale. Technological advancements and geographical discoveries sparked a new era where maritime trade routes were established, linking China to Europe, Africa, and other regions. Trade via the Silk Road and these sea routes brought enormous wealth to China, boosting the economy.

The Ming Dynasty also saw the implementation of state-controlled industries, ensuring the stability of supply for crucial commodities like salt and silk. This economic system, interventionist yet providing room for private commerce, nurtured the prosperity that the Ming Dynasty was known for.

9.6. Ancient Economic Wisdom in Modern Guise

From the Zhou coins to the jiaozi of the Song and Yuan dynasties, and to the maritime trade excelling during the Ming Dynasty, ancient China's economy and its underlying principles hold vital lessons for financial prosperity. Bound by ethics, moderated by wisdom, marked by innovation, and periodically disrupted by overreach, these lessons hold as true today as thousands of years ago. When navigating the global economic landscape of the 21st century, a look back at our ancestral wisdom might be worth more than a passing glance.

Chapter 10. Middle-Aged Reflections on Wealth: From Feudalism to Renaissance

It was a period of dramatic shifts, as the Middle Ages transitioned into the Renaissance, finally relinquishing its tightly held grasp on the world for almost a thousand years. As the feudal lens gradually dimmed and the bright rays of the Renaissance began to envelop society, the perception and ethos of wealth underwent a profound transformation.

10.1. The Feudal Economy and its Notions about Wealth

Before exploring the transition, it's essential to understand the feudal system that shaped the society and economy during the Middle Ages. It was a simple yet rigid social structure with the monarch at the top followed by the nobility, and then the commoners. This rigid stratification greatly influenced the accumulation of wealth.

Land was the primary means of acquiring and maintaining wealth. Being in possession of land elevated one's status and guaranteed sustenance, as it was a source of food, timber, and other resources. The majority of the populace – the serfs – did not own the land but were tied to it, working for the lords in exchange for protection and the right to work a portion of the land for their own benefit. The inherent challenge here was the concentration of wealth in the hands of the few, creating a highly unequal society.

In addition to agriculture, trade slowly began to develop during the latter period of the Middle Ages, spurring growth in the economy. This budding mercantile system, however, was still subject to the power of the feudal lords, as merchants required protection and often had to pay taxes or tributes to conduct their business.

10.2. Transitioning to a Monetized Economy

The late Middle Ages and early Renaissance marked the beginning of substantive change in societal structure and wealth accumulation. As cities and trade grew more prevalent, so did the use of money. Rather than exchanging goods or services in kind, standardized currency started to gain popularity. This transition to a monetized economy provided a more efficient and flexible means of trade, fostering a new class of merchants and craftsmen who had the power to shape the economy and amass wealth independently.

Despite the growth of monetization, land remained a significant marker of wealth due to the sustenance and resources it offered. As the existing wealth was primarily invested in land and material wealth, the shift to liquid asset forms had difficulty shaking the established order. But as trade routes expanded and commerce flourished, liquid wealth became an increasingly important standard.

10.3. The Advent of Banking and Financial Institutions

In conjunction with the growing importance of cash, the late Middle Ages saw the advent of the first foundations of the banking system. Banking had its roots in Italy, nurturing a whole new way of transacting, which dramatically affected the accumulation and amassing of wealth.

Primarily, financial institutions began offering services like loans and changing money, pioneering interest-based economic transactions rather than physical trade. Loans, especially, became crucial as they gave individuals and businesses the opportunity to advance ambitions they otherwise would not have been able to afford. The banking system's development incorporated a new dimension into wealth creation and marked the beginning of looking at wealth beyond tangible assets.

10.4. The Birth of Capitalism and Renaissance Humanism

The Renaissance, in stark contrast to the preceding Middle Ages, was a period of renewed focus on individual capabilities and human potential. This humanist philosophy emphasized the value of the individual, challenging the strictly hierarchical social structures defining wealth in the feudal system. This birthed capitalism, an economic system where labor became tradable and valuable, leading to a sophisticated interplay of wealth generation and distribution.

For the first time, wealth was subject to merit rather than birthright. A serf could evolve into a wealthy merchant or a skilled craftsman based purely on talents, efforts, and fortunes. The economic systems became more fluid, providing a fertile grounds for social mobility.

In conclusion, the period of the Middle Ages to the Renaissance represented a significant shift in wealth accumulation, signaling a departure from a concentrated land-based economy to more diverse forms of wealth. The societal structure also saw drastic changes, leading to a more equitable distribution of wealth. Lastly and most notably, it marked the debut of banking, which not only transformed commerce but changed forever the processes and perception of wealth accumulation. This period served as a catalyst for the modern-day understanding of wealth, bearing crucial lessons for maintaining and sustaining financial prosperity.

Chapter 11. The East's Affluence: Indian and Persian Major Trade Routes

Trade has been the lifeblood of civilizations, leading to the flow of goods, ideas, culture, and economic wealth from one region to another. The Indian subcontinent and Persia have played monumental roles in this lively exchange, developing, maintaining, and leveraging major trade routes that have significantly contributed to the East's affluence.

11.1. Ancient Indian Trade Routes

India's strategic location along the Silk Road, Spice Route, and other lucrative trade routes meant it was both a final destination and a conduit for a wide variety of goods. From the time of the Indus Valley Civilization, trade was embedded in Indian society.

The Harappans, who thrived around 2500 BCE, were among the first to establish a comprehensive trade network within the Indian subcontinent. They engaged in maritime trade, with Mesopotamia being a notable trading partner. Excavations of ancient Mesopotamian sites have unearthed Indus valley artifacts, while Indus cities like Lothal and Dholavira have revealed Mesopotamian imports, pointing to a robust trade relationship.

By the time of the Mauryan Empire (322–185 BCE), India's internal trade network had expanded. Primarily, trade traversed the Ganges River, where goods like spices, textiles, grains, and precious stones flowed between cities and port towns.

International maritime trade grew under the Mauryans, with routes to Southeast Asia and Egypt recorded in texts like the Periplus of the

Erythraean Sea. Additionally, the Silk Route, stretching from China to Europe, saw Indian traders acting as intermediaries, with Indian towns becoming important junctions along the way.

11.2. Persian Trade Routes

Persia, known today as Iran, was another key player in ancient trade. The Royal Road, arguably the most influential trade route in Persian history, was constructed during the reign of King Darius I of the Achaemenid Empire.

Stretching over 2,600 kilometers, from Susa to Sardis, the Royal Road allowed swift communication and movement of goods across the empire, vital to sustaining the Achaemenid bureaucracy and military.

Persia benefitted greatly from its position along the Silk Road, giving it access to the Chinese, Indian, and Mediterranean economies. Persian cities became multicultural hubs where goods, ideas, and cultures intermingled.

11.3. Impact of Trade Routes on Economic Prosperity

Trade routes had an undeniable impact on the economic prosperity of India and Persia. These routes not only facilitated the exchange of goods but also the spread of technology, knowledge, religion, and culture - a broader yet vital aspect of trade.

In India, the profits from both internal and international trade led to the creation of thriving urban centres like Pataliputra and helped fund magnificent architectural projects like the Mauryan pillar capitals.

In Persia, the wealth generated from trade facilitated grand city development, fostered arts and culture, and even helped sustain the military might of the Achaemenid Empire. It allowed Persian culture to influence a vast geographical area.

11.4. Cultural Exchange through Trade

Trade was not solely about the exchange of goods. It also emboldened the exchange and diffusion of cultures, religions, and innovations.

In India, Buddhism flourished during the Mauryan period, partly due to the patronage of Emperor Ashoka, who sent Buddhist missionaries across the trade routes to propagate the message of Buddhism. This led to the establishment of Buddhism in Southeast Asia and Central Asia.

In Persia, while Zoroastrianism and later Islam were the major religions, the position of Persia on the Silk Road brought it into contact with diverse cultures and religions. This resulted in Persian culture becoming highly cosmopolitan and influential.

These thriving trade routes in India and Persia indubitably contributed to the East's wealth and cultural affluence. They stood witness to an intermingling of cultures and economies, highlighting the profundity of long-established principles in wealth creation and prosperity: open borders, free trade, and cultural exchange. Indeed, by exploring these eastern trade networks, we glean timeless insights into wealth accumulation and economic resilience.

Chapter 12. Infusing Ancient Wisdom into Contemporary Financial Management

Engaging with our financial world, we may often feel swamped by convoluted jargon and the dizzying speed of technological advancements. Yet, simplifying the analysis of your finances and inculcating time-proven money-management skills can lead to lasting prosperity. Let's delve into the ancient wisdom to learn the foundational framework required to navigate the contemporary world of finance.

12.1. Money Matters of Antiquity

In ancient civilizations, where complex financial systems like ours did not exist, people still found ways to prosper. One key method was simple – they saved. Ancient Egyptians, for instance, stored surplus grain from bountiful harvests in communal granaries for leaner times, illustrating an early form of saving. This lesson in preparing for the future underscores the significance of saving, a principle that holds vast relevance in managing personal finances today.

Moreover, ancient civilizations understood the relevance of diversifying assets to balance risk. In ancient Mesopotamia, the oldest known civilization, wealth was not confined to grain or livestock alone. It also included land, slaves, precious metals, and craft goods, implying a diversified approach to asset accumulation. Today, monetary investments span across various asset classes such as stocks, bonds, real estate, or precious metals, a concept that echoes the diversification strategy from ancient times.

12.2. The Art of Budgeting

Ancient Rome provides a vibrant example of early budgeting. The Roman government would devise a financial plan each year, detailing the proposed income and expenditure across various sectors. This measure ensured balance in the realms of military, civil governance, and public works, allowing the empire to thrive. A contemporary equivalent is an individual's yearly budget, which meticulously allocates income towards necessities, savings, and discretionary expenditures, fostering financial stability and growth.

12.3. Managing Credit and Debt

The use of credit and debt isn't a new phenomenon. Ancient Sumer saw the first recorded use of credit, where farmers would borrow seeds and pay back the loan—with interest—after harvest. The insight here is to leverage credit as a tool for growth but to manage loan repayment efficiently. In the modern context, borrowing responsibly and maintaining a good credit score are paramount to financial health.

Common folk in ancient societies often fell into the debt trap during famines or emergencies. Debt forgiveness, or jubilees, held by Mesopotamian kings set a precedent by creating a bailout plan for the financially distressed. It sheds light on the significance of managing uncontrollable debt, which resonates today in bankruptcy laws and debt consolidation strategies.

12.4. Investing Wisely

When it comes to investment, one can draw lessons from the ancient Middle East. Merchants traded textiles, oils, and precious metals across the Silk Road, investing labor and resources into products that would yield profits. This practice exemplifies the importance of allocating resources into avenues that offer substantial return potential.

Today, this wisdom translates into investing in viable stocks, bonds, and other asset classes. Similar to those ancient traders, modern investors take on a level of risk, speculating that the value of their assets will increase over time.

12.5. Embracing the Value of Hard Work

From the labor-intensive agricultural era to the hard-working tradesmen of medieval times, the principle of toiling for wealth has always been instilled in society. There is no stand-in for the value for hard work and dedication. Balancing multiple jobs, upskilling for better job prospects, or tirelessly nurturing a start-up concept—all reflect the spirit of laboring for monetary success, a lesson deeply ingrained in history.

To summarize, by extracting wisdom from the annals of history and adopting time-honored finance lessons, it's possible to create a solid foundation for managing personal finances in the present day. Remember, the path to financial prosperity is a marathon, not a sprint. It hinges on slowly but surely building wealth over time, planning for the unexpected, diversifying assets, and most essentially, cultivating the discipline and patience that money management requires.

www.ingramcontent.com/pod-product-compliance
Lightning Source LLC
Chambersburg PA
CBHW060901260726
48661CB00008B/3386